What Was Ellis Island?

What Was Ellis Island?

by Patricia Brennan Demuth
illustrated by David Groff

Grosset & Dunlap
An Imprint of Penguin Group (USA) LLC

For Jahsiah Courage Demuth,
who's simply terrific—PBD

For my wonderful mother, Eva Groff, whose
parents came to America via Ellis Island on their
honeymoon and never looked back—DG

GROSSET & DUNLAP
Published by the Penguin Group
Penguin Group (USA) LLC, 375 Hudson Street, New York, New York 10014, USA

USA | Canada | UK | Ireland | Australia | New Zealand | India | South Africa | China

penguin.com
A Penguin Random House Company

If you purchased this book without a cover, you should be aware that this book is stolen property. It was reported as "unsold and destroyed" to the publisher, and neither the author nor the publisher has received any payment for this "stripped book."

Penguin supports copyright. Copyright fuels creativity, encourages diverse voices, promotes free speech, and creates a vibrant culture. Thank you for buying an authorized edition of this book and for complying with copyright laws by not reproducing, scanning, or distributing any part of it in any form without permission. You are supporting writers and allowing Penguin to continue to publish books for every reader.

The publisher does not have any control over and does not assume any responsibility for author or third-party websites or their content.

Text copyright © 2014 by Patricia Brennan. Illustrations copyright © 2014 by Penguin Group (USA) LLC. Cover illustration copyright © 2014 by Penguin Group (USA) LLC. All rights reserved. Published by Grosset & Dunlap, a division of Penguin Young Readers Group, 345 Hudson Street, New York, New York 10014. GROSSET & DUNLAP is a trademark of Penguin Group (USA) LLC. Printed in the USA.

Library of Congress Cataloging-in-Publication Data is available.

ISBN 978-0-448-47915-6   10 9

Contents

What Was Ellis Island? 1
A Scrap of Land 8
Leaving Home 22
Testing 34
Stuck on the Island 47
New Lives 62
The Open Door Slams Shut 76
Back from Ruins 84
Ellis Island Today 96
Timelines 104
Bibliography 106

What Was Ellis Island?

The Island of Hope.

Many people thought of Ellis Island that way. Millions and millions of immigrants came to this tiny island off New York City from 1892 to 1954. Ellis Island was their first stop in America. It had to be. Until they passed through there, newcomers could not set foot inside the United States.

Immigrants are people who leave their homeland behind, hoping for a better life. The immigrants stopping at Ellis Island mostly came from all over Europe. Many were escaping from terrible problems. Food was scarce in their homeland. There were no jobs. They were treated badly because of their religion. Although poor in money, immigrants were rich in hope. America meant freedom, jobs, and safety.

"America was on everyone's lips," said one boy who came from Poland. "We talked about America. We dreamt about America. We all had one wish—to be in America."

The immigrants traveled across the Atlantic Ocean, crammed into ships that generally took seven to ten days to reach America. After hard days at sea, they entered New York Harbor and caught sight of two small islands. One was Liberty Island, where the Statue of Liberty held up a flaming torch. A poem at the base of the statue welcomed the immigrants to America.

The second was Ellis Island, just a few hundred yards away. The greeting there was not as friendly. Ellis Island was a testing center run by the US government. Its purpose was to check immigrants and weed out the sick and unfit. The vast majority of immigrants passed the tests. They were free to go ashore and start their new life.

But over the years, at least 250,000 immigrants failed the tests. Those unlucky ones were not allowed into the United States. Sent back on the ships, they returned to where they had

come from. This earned Ellis Island its other name: the Island of Tears.

The Statue of Liberty

For over 125 years, the Statue of Liberty has stood tall as a symbol of freedom in New York Harbor. The statue was a gift of friendship from the people of France to the people of the United States.

In 1903, part of a poem by Emma Lazarus entitled "The New Colossus" was inscribed on the base. Its famous last lines are a ringing welcome from America to its immigrants:

"Give me your tired, your poor,

Your huddled masses yearning to breathe free,

The wretched refuse of your teeming shore.

Send these, the homeless, tempest-tossed to me,

I lift my lamp beside the golden door!"

CHAPTER 1
A Scrap of Land

At first, Ellis Island was just a small scrap of empty land, a little over three acres. It barely stuck out of the water at high tide. The local Native Americans called it Gull Island. Seagulls were the only creatures that lived there.

Around the time of the Revolutionary War, a farmer named Samuel Ellis bought the land. Although he later sold it, the island would keep his name.

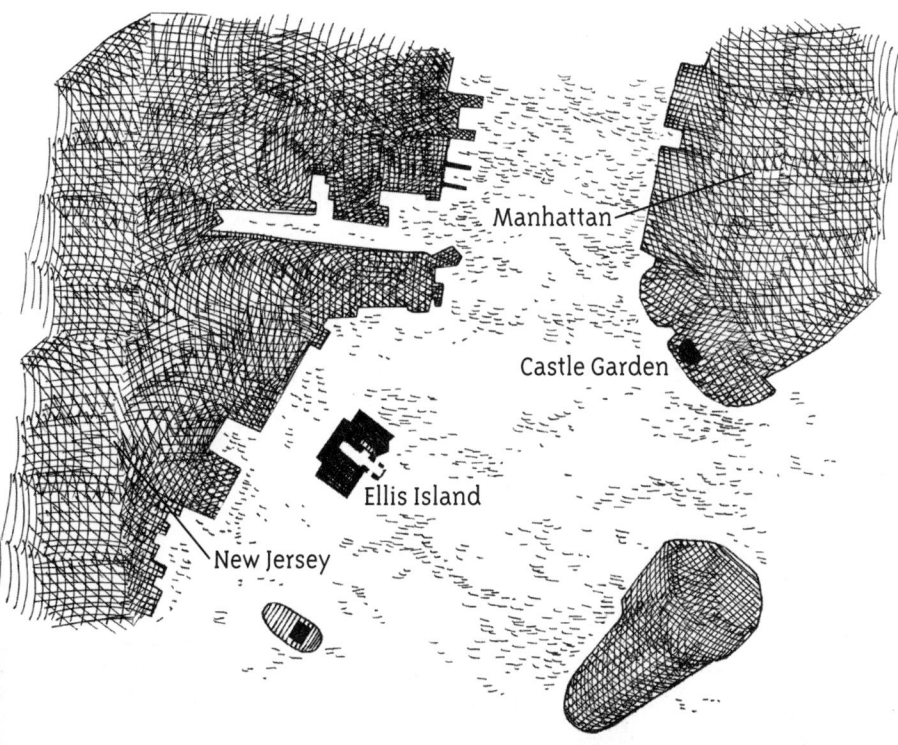

Then, in 1808, the US government became the island's new owner. For a long while the island was only used for storing guns to protect the harbor. No one dreamed that one day Ellis Island would become the gateway to America for many waves of immigrants.

In fact, for most of the 1800s, the US government did not control immigration. There was an "open door policy." That meant that any immigrant who wanted to could move there. The states were in charge of keeping track of the newcomers.

The flow of immigrants remained fairly slow until the mid 1800s. Then a huge wave of people started to pour into the country. Nine out of ten came from Ireland, England, or Germany.

The state of New York alone admitted eight million immigrants from 1855 to 1890. They came through a station called Castle Garden at the tip of New York City.

Finally, in 1890, the federal government took over immigration from the individual states. It wanted to start testing newcomers to make sure they were free of disease and able to support themselves. Where would it build the first immigration station? Ellis Island seemed the perfect place. It was located in New York Harbor, where so many ships from Europe already docked.

Yet the island was too tiny for the job. No problem. The island was made bigger! Engineers built a seawall away from the island. It was set deep into the harbor floor. They filled the area in between the wall and the island with tons of landfill—dirt, sand, and stone. At that time, vast tunnels, miles long, were being dug in New York City for a subway system. A lot of the landfill for Ellis Island came from the dirt shoveled out to make way for the subways!

Ellis Island greeted its first immigrants on New Year's Day 1892. An Irish girl named Annie Moore was the first to step foot on the island. Just fifteen years old, she had brought her two younger brothers to America. Their parents were already there. So the three children made the long voyage by themselves. Today a statue of brave Annie stands on the island.

Then, only five years after opening, the buildings on Ellis Island burned to the ground. Plans for rebuilding started immediately. The old buildings had been made of wood. The new ones were made of red brick and stone. Now Ellis Island was completely fireproof.

Right from the start, Ellis Island was swamped with more people than it could handle. During its first year, Ellis Island admitted nearly 450,000 immigrants. And the numbers kept growing. In 1898, a second island, also made of landfill, was added. Still, Ellis Island was too small to handle the crush of people. So, in 1906, a third—and final—island was added.

Annie Moore (1877–1924)

Annie Moore had a special fifteenth birthday on January 1, 1892. She was the first immigrant to land at Ellis Island. Officials handed the "rosy-cheeked Irish girl" a ten-dollar gold piece for the honor. Leaving County Cork in Ireland twelve days earlier, Annie had traveled in steerage on the steamship *Nevada*.

She brought her two younger brothers, Anthony, eleven, and Philip, seven, with her.

Despite her happy arrival, Annie faced the hard life of many immigrants. She settled with her parents in the Lower East Side of New York City and never moved more than a few blocks away. Marrying a bakery clerk, Annie gave birth to eleven children, though five died as infants. Annie died in 1924 at age forty-seven.

Now complete, Ellis Island was really three islands in one. From 3.3 acres, it had grown to 27.5 acres!

The island was like a separate city in the harbor. There were thirty-three buildings, including a hospital, laundry, and power plant to make electricity. There were places to exchange foreign money, buy railroad tickets, and send telegrams. But the biggest and most important building by far was the Main Building. A massive structure, it was where all immigrants went when they first stepped on dry land—and where they found out if the United States would become their new home . . . or if they would be sent back to their native land.

Early Irish Immigrants

Between 1845 and 1855, more than one million Irish immigrants arrived in America. Back in Ireland, blight was ruining the potato crops. Without their staple food, a million Irish starved to death. The terrible time became known as the Potato Famine. By 1855, Ireland had lost one-fourth of its population to death or emigration.

In the United States, the Irish still faced hard times. Prejudice against their Catholic religion was widespread in a country that was mostly Protestant. Shops and factories posted signs that said "No Irish Need Apply." Irish workers survived by shoveling coal, unloading ships, and cleaning yards.

The huge wave of incoming Irish transformed the populations of New York City and Boston. In 1847, when the first Irish masses arrived, New York City had a total population of 372,000. Nearly double that number of Irish—about 650,000— flooded into the city during the next ten years.

CHAPTER 2
Leaving Home

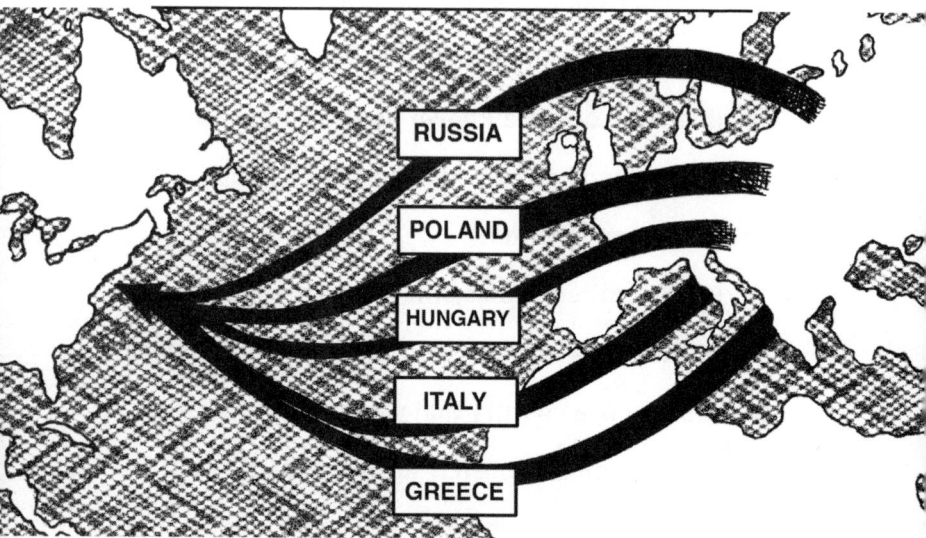

A major shift in US immigration happened at the end of the 1800s. Until then, most immigrants had come from northern and western Europe. But at the end of the century, immigrants from southern and eastern Europe flooded into America. Most came from Italy, Greece, Russia, Hungary, and Poland.

What made so many people leave their homeland? America was growing fast. Some people came for jobs in all the new factories in big cities. Some came to get cheap land out west.

But terrible hardship drove most immigrants across the ocean to America. Millions were so poor, families didn't have enough to eat or any way to earn a living. Some governments oppressed their people. In Italy, there was famine as well as natural disasters—earthquakes, tidal waves, and the eruption of Mt. Etna. "I do not want to raise my children in [Italy] any longer," one mother told her son. "I don't want no famine. I don't want no poverty. . . . [If we go to America] at least we'll eat."

Many immigrants suffered because of their religion. In Russia, hundreds of Jews were beaten and killed in attacks called *pogroms.* Thousands of Jews were left homeless when their houses were set on fire and their villages destroyed. Mary Antin, a young Jewish girl who escaped to America in 1894, later wrote about the terror back in Russia. Mobs "attacked [Jewish families] with knives and clubs and scythes and axes," she said. "People

Mt. Etna

who saw such things never smiled anymore, and sometimes their hair turned white in a day."

Scraping up enough money for the fare to America was not easy. Often a family had to move in stages. The father usually went first. He worked in the United States and saved until he had enough money to send for his family.

When the time to go finally came, few could believe it. Many had never been away from their villages before. Now they were crossing an ocean three thousand miles wide. They were headed for a country where people spoke a different language, wore different clothes, and ate different food. "Going to America then was almost like going to the moon," said immigrant Golda Meir, who later became prime minister of Israel.

What should they bring from home to start a new life? Not very much! Immigrants could only bring what they could carry—or wear. As a result, some wore all their clothes in layer upon layer. They had to leave behind their furniture and other possessions. In America, they would be starting all over.

The travelers were leaving behind family and friends, often forever. One immigrant recalled saying good-bye to his father in Italy: "He said, 'Make yourself courage.' And that was the last I ever saw my father."

Immigrants made their way to the steamships any way they could, even on foot. At the docks, they couldn't board until they were vaccinated (given shots against disease) and checked for lice. They also had to answer several questions: *What is your name, age, and place of birth? What is your height and race? Have you ever been to prison?* The steamship companies wrote down their answers in huge logs, called *manifests*. They screened immigrants with care. If anybody was sent back from Ellis Island, the steamship companies had to pay for the return trip.

The Atlantic voyage took about ten days. However, bad weather could make it twice as long.

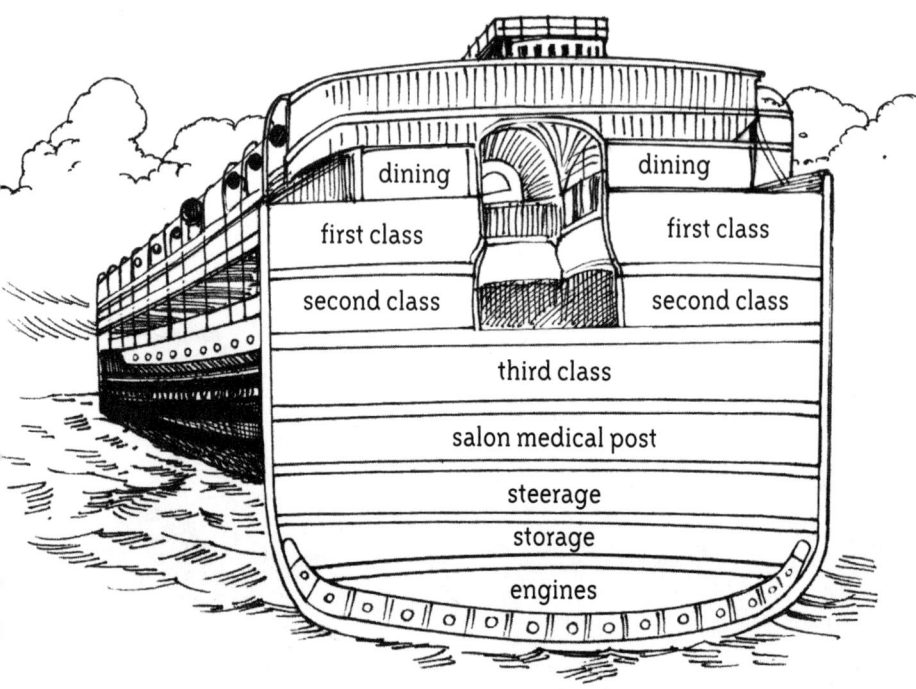

Immigrants usually could only afford a ticket in the rough area at the bottom of the ship, near the steering equipment. It was called *steerage*.

On the fancy upper decks of the ships, there were cabins. But in steerage there were just rows of bunk beds. A thousand or more men, women, and children were packed together. It was dark and damp below sea level, with no portholes to let in fresh air. Food was dished out of pails. To wash up, people had to use cold salt water from a faucet. "Most immigrants lie in their [bunks] for most of the voyage, in a [dulled state] caused by the foul air," said a government report.

Immigrants rejoiced when at last they entered New York Harbor. Edward Corsi was just ten when he came to America in 1907. He later wrote, "Mother and father lifted up the babies so that they too could see . . . the Statue of Liberty."

Next stop: Ellis Island.

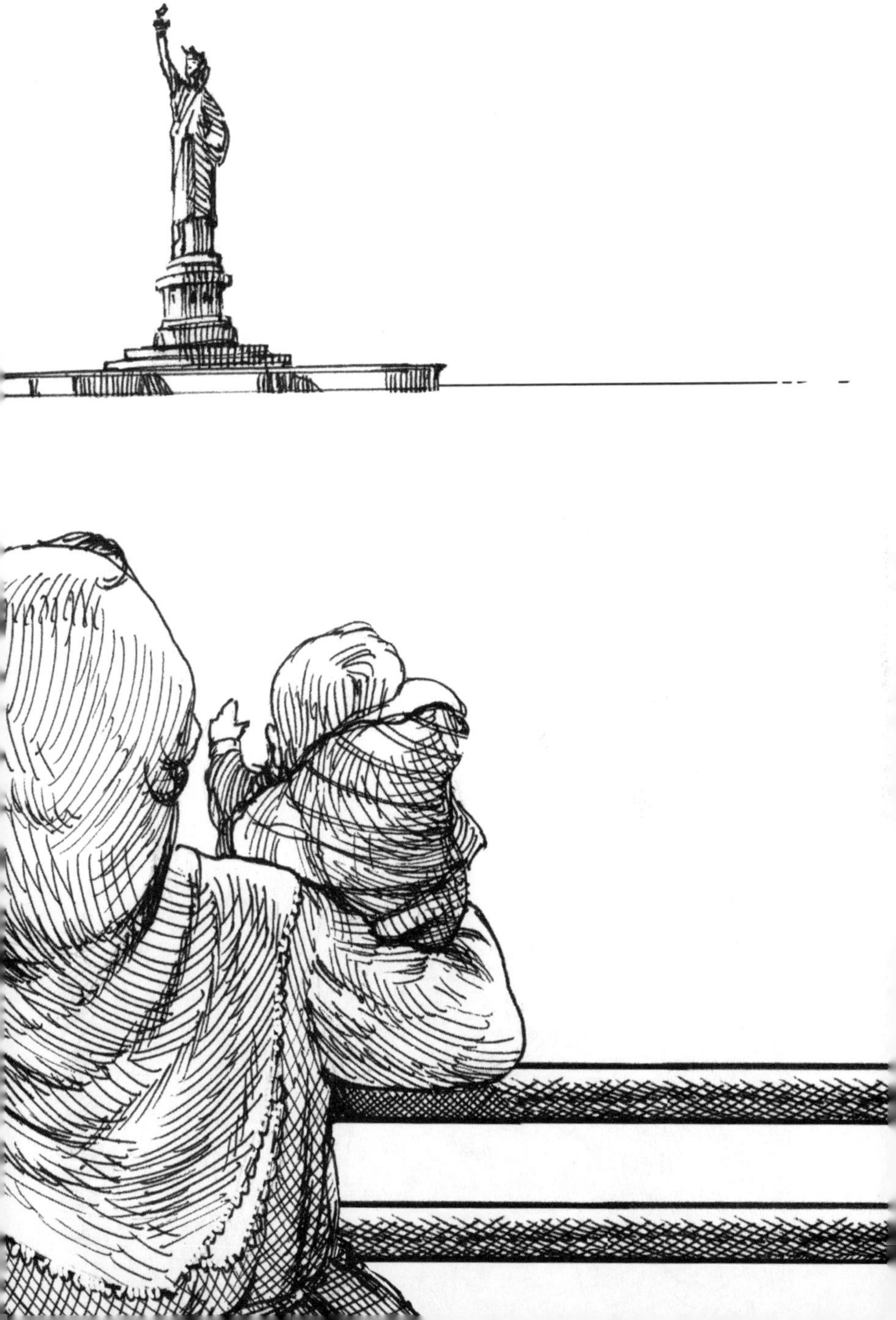

CHAPTER 3
Testing

Once the steamships docked in New York City, the immigrants in steerage were put on ferries for Ellis Island, a mile away. Usually groups of a thousand arrived on the island at one time.

It was scary and confusing for the immigrants.

They struggled off the boat under the load of their heavy bags and trunks. Officials in uniforms shouted orders that most of the new arrivals couldn't understand. They were herded toward a huge redbrick structure, the Main Building. "I never saw such a big building—the size of it!" said an immigrant from Russia. "According to the houses I left in my town, this was like a whole city . . . in one building."

Inside, the immigrants had to walk up a large, steep stairway. At the top were doctors with pieces of blue chalk. They were looking to see if the immigrants seemed healthy. Did they limp? Were they coughing? Were their eyes red? What about skin sores? If there was a problem, the doctor put a chalk letter on the person's back. *H* stood for heart, *E* for eyes, and so on.

Chalk marks meant trouble! Marked immigrants were pulled aside and led away for further tests. Children with the marks were taken from their families. One immigrant recalled the heartbreaking scene of a sick child taken from its mother. "The mother was holding the child and singing. All of a sudden, a doctor and two nurses took the child away. The mother couldn't speak English. And they're talking to her in English. They were saying that the child had to go to the hospital."

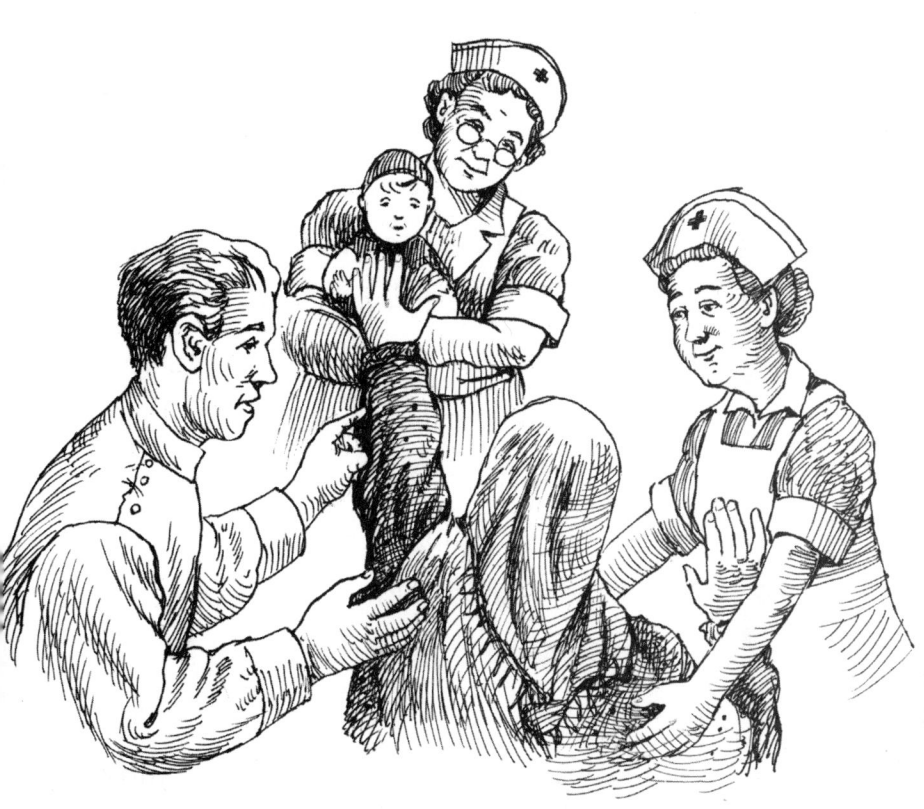

Immigrants without chalk marks waited in line for a quick medical checkup. By far the worst part was the "buttonhook test," the name for the eye exam. A buttonhook was a small curved tool used for buttoning women's shoes. But doctors at Ellis Island used it for turning eyelids inside out. They were checking for *trachoma*, a terrible eye disease that could lead to blindness. Trachoma spread quickly and easily. So it became one of the most likely medical reasons for sending immigrants home.

Following the medical check, immigrants entered the Great Hall to await their next test. This giant room looked like a maze of rows, separated by iron rails. The noise inside was deafening as a mix of languages bounced off the high ceiling overhead.

For those in line, the noise wasn't as bad as their fear of the test ahead—a legal interview. They knew that wrong answers could get them *deported*—sent back.

When their names were called, immigrants went to stand before inspectors seated at high desks. Spread out on the desks were the huge pages from the ships' manifests. Inspectors fired off a list of questions: *Where did you last live? Are you married? Do you have children? What is your occupation? Do you have family in America?*

Interpreters stood nearby to help. Ellis Island had interpreters for many languages. They translated back and forth, from the inspector to the immigrant. It was a deep relief for immigrants to have someone understand what they were saying. Interpreters could explain confusing questions, too.

Even the question *What is your name?* had no simple answer. Foreign names were long and unfamiliar to inspectors. They sometimes made mistakes in spelling them. As a result, some immigrants arrived from home with one name and left Ellis Island with another. A few inspectors may have shortened names on purpose. The name *Finkelstein* might be changed to *Finkel* or *Stein*. *Goldensternweiss* became *Gold* or *Weiss*. Some immigrants changed their own names to make them more "American."

Another question was very tricky. *Do you have a job waiting for you in America?* A *yes* answer would prove that immigrants could make a living and not end up on public aid. But the right answer was *no*. By law, American businesses could not bring over immigrants to work in their factories or mines. Why? For years, crooked companies had taken advantage of immigrants by paying their way to America. Then immigrants ended up trapped in hard, low-paying jobs for years.

How much money did you bring? Immigrants had to arrive at Ellis Island with twenty or twenty-five dollars, depending on the year. Penniless immigrants were more likely to be a burden on society.

Can you read? This question was not asked until 1917. That year a new law was passed to keep out illiterate immigrants. *Illiterate* means "unable to read or write." Now immigrants had to read forty words of text in English or some other language. Some found ways around the new law. One boy coached his illiterate mother to open the book the inspector gave her and recite the Lord's Prayer. Hearing the mother "reading" smoothly, the inspector passed her!

Help in passing the tests sometimes even came from the interpreters. A number of them had come through Ellis Island themselves. One interpreter named Edward Ferro wrote that some of the "softhearted" interpreters "hated to see people being deported." They sometimes reworded the immigrants' answers in a way "to benefit the [person] and not the government."

When the interview ended, the tests were finally over! At least they were for approximately eight out of ten immigrants. Those who passed were free to leave. On average, their stay at Ellis

Island lasted three to five hours. But those who failed were detained. Who knew for how long? They could be stuck on the island for days, weeks . . . even months.

Mail-Order Brides

During the legal interview, immigrants were asked who paid their fare to the United States. Thousands of women, called "mail-order brides," had an unusual answer. Their tickets were paid by *future* husbands, men they had never seen! Mail-order brides were so called because they became engaged by mail to men living in the United States who were from the same native country. To find a bride, the men placed ads in their homeland newspapers. A woman responded by sending a letter about herself, along with a picture. It was a risky way for a young woman to get to America. But thousands wanted to leave their homelands badly enough to take the chance.

CHAPTER 4
Stuck on the Island

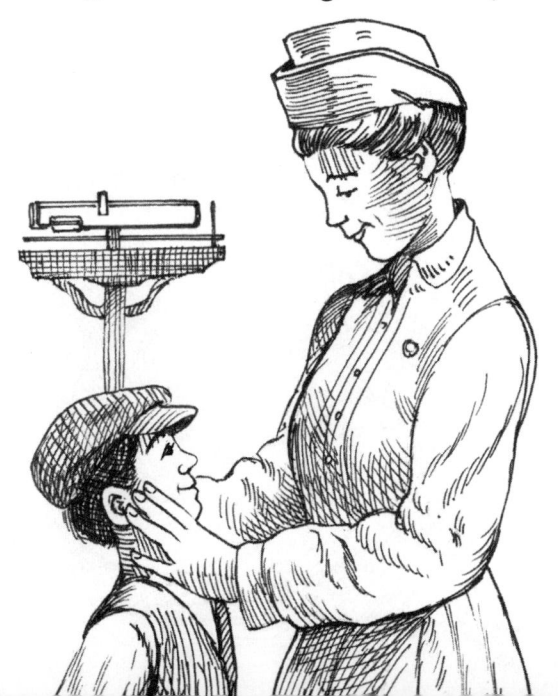

The sick were taken to the Ellis Island Hospital. Opened in 1902, it was the most caring place on the island. Nurses went out of their way to comfort patients, especially scared children separated from their parents. "'Ladies in white,' we used to call [the nurses]," said an immigrant. "They were very nice. I mean, they talked to the children. They stroked their hair. And they touched their cheeks and held our hands."

Treatment at the hospital was free of charge. Tens of thousands regained their health and then were able to enter America. Hundreds of babies were born there, too, becoming instant citizens.

Immigrants who had given wrong answers for the legal test were held for more questioning. They had to appear before a Board of Special Inquiry, made up of three men. It was like going to court. "I was never so frightened in my life," said one immigrant. "My whole future was in their hands. And I could hardly keep my arms and legs from shaking."

And then there were women who had come to America alone. By law, they could not leave Ellis Island until a male relative or sponsor came for them. (A sponsor promised to take care of a woman until she found a home and job.) An interpreter named Frank Martocci described the trouble that the women faced. "[Sometimes] the man could not be located," he said. "Perhaps he had died, or moved, or the [letters] hadn't reached him—who knows?" If no one came, stranded females had to return to their homeland. "There was no way of soothing these heartbroken women," said Martocci.

At times, aid societies came to the rescue and offered the women places to stay and help finding jobs. Over forty aid societies—such as the Salvation Army, Red Cross, and YWCA—had volunteers on Ellis Island. Some groups were even given office space.

Such kindness accounted for why some detainees left Ellis Island with good memories. Free food was another reason. Immigrants were fed three meals a day in a dining room that seated a thousand people. They had their first taste of American dishes such as sandwiches, corn on the cob, Jell-O, and ice cream.

They also enjoyed comforts like hot running water. A Greek immigrant recalled his first shower on Ellis Island with delight. "The hot water [was] washing away the sweat and dust and grime of the steerage. . . . I washed away the Old World. I washed away all the hatred and injustice and cruelty I had known."

Even so, being detained could be deeply stressful. Overcrowding on the island was partly the reason. In 1907, the busiest year, nearly 1.25 *million* newcomers arrived at Ellis Island. On a single day that year, nine ships unloaded 11,500 men, women, and children.

At night, immigrants slept in large packed rooms that looked like giant wire cages. Men stayed in their own dorms, women and children in others. Bedding often ran short. One newcomer in 1913 recalled shivering all night without a blanket and listening to dreams in "a dozen different languages."

During the day, immigrants waited in large wire cells known as "pens." Each was built to hold six hundred people. Yet often more than a thousand immigrants had to jam inside. There they waited . . . and waited.

The staff suffered, too, under a heavy workload. During the peak years of 1903–1914, Ellis Island employed between 500 and 800 workers—and still it wasn't enough. Besides inspectors and translators, there were baggage handlers, doctors and nurses, railroad ticket agents, cooks, cleaning staff, clerks, and more. The laundry washed 3,000 sheets and towels a day. And the kitchen struggled to make meals for different appetites. Many Italians did not like potatoes; many Irish did not eat spaghetti. Jews could not eat foods that weren't kosher. (In 1911, a kosher kitchen was put in.)

Inspector Fiorello La Guardia recalled working seven days a week. "Immigrants were pouring in at the average rate of five thousand a day," he said. Work "was a constant grind from the moment we got into our uniforms early in the morning until the last minute before we left . . ." As a result, tempers sometimes flared. And immigrants got the worst of it.

But by far the most heartbreaking turn of events for immigrants was being forced to return to their homelands. Most had little or nothing to return to. They had sold everything they owned in order to reach America.

Fortunately, Ellis Island deported only 2 percent of its immigrants. The rest were handed the grand prize—their landing cards. They had proved they were "clearly and beyond a doubt entitled to land." At last, they were free to go ashore.

Immigrant Louis Sage wrote of his exit from Ellis Island: "I had my landing card in my pocket with my hand clutched around it. I never took my hand out of that pocket until the ferry that took us off the Island landed in New York."

Their journey to the United States was over. A new journey was now beginning.

The Kissing Post

As they left Ellis Island, immigrants were often greeted by family members they hadn't seen for years. The spot where these reunions took place was fondly called the "kissing post."

An immigrant from Italy, Regina Rogatta, recalled the moment she and her brothers and sister saw their father. He came running and "squatted on his knees with his arms outstretched, and the five of us ran into his arms." Her father said, "We're all together now. We'll never be apart again."

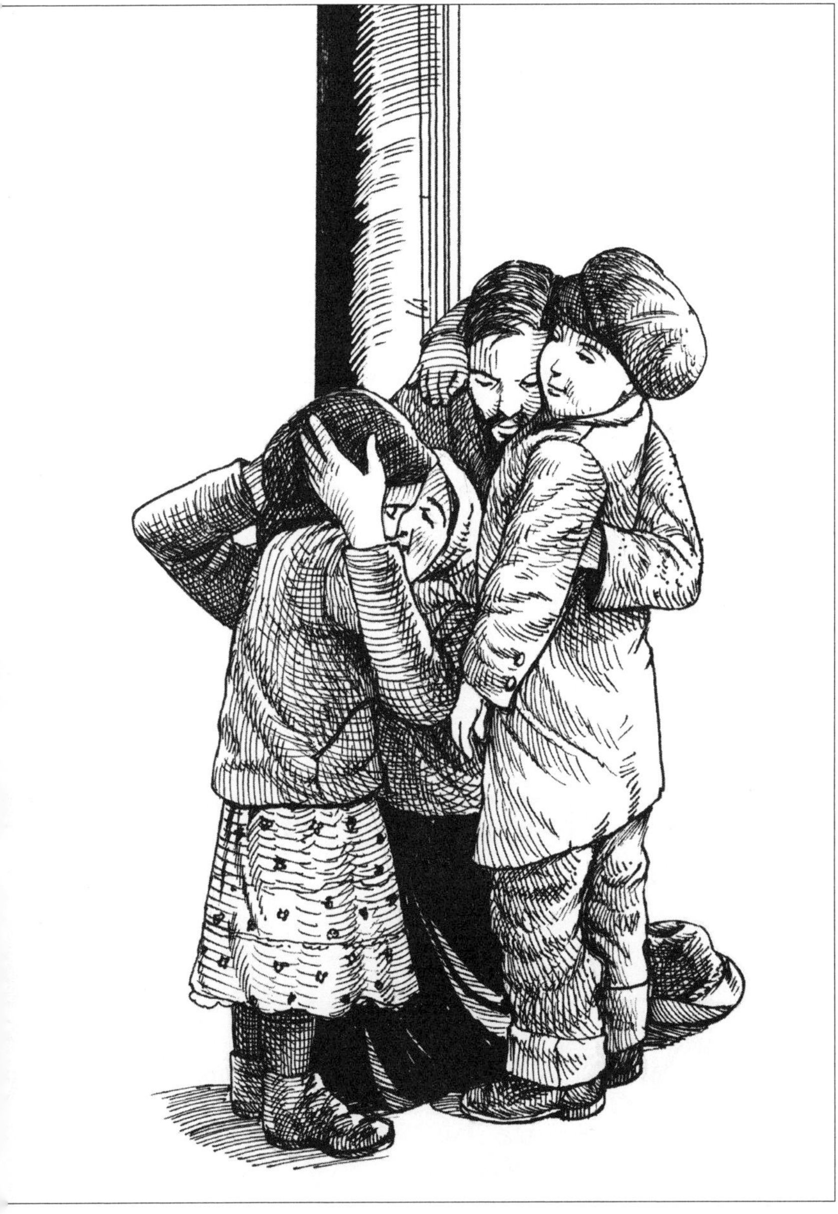

CHAPTER 5
New Lives

When they left Ellis Island, immigrants fanned out across America to start new lives. Their huge numbers transformed the face of the nation. In 1820, the US population was about ten million. By 1920, it was ten times greater, largely due to the yearly inflow of people from Europe.

Millions of immigrants moved to the vast plains out west. In the late 1800s, the government gave away land to homesteaders who agreed to farm it. When the free land ran out, railroad companies sold millions more acres at very low prices. They wanted towns to be built along their rail lines. And immigrants were eager to build them.

Most immigrants, however, headed for the big cities to work in factories and mills. At the turn of the century, America's economy was booming. Across the nation, bridges, skyscrapers, and rail lines were being built. In 1913, new cars were pouring off assembly lines.

The steel industry drove the boom. And immigrants supplied the manpower to make steel. More than half of US steelworkers were immigrants. They worked twelve-hour days, seven days a week. Steel tycoon Andrew Carnegie gave his workers only one day off—on the Fourth of July. On the other 364 days, his crews were on the job, working furnaces heated to about three thousand degrees. "Hard, I guess it's hard," said one immigrant steelworker. "I lost forty pounds the first three months I came into the business. It sweats the life out of a man."

Fiorello La Guardia (1882–1947)

La Guardia's Italian father was Catholic and his immigrant mother from Austria-Hungary was Jewish. Able to speak five languages, La Guardia worked as an interpreter at Ellis Island for three years while going to law school. He was known as one of the kindest officials on the island.

After law school, La Guardia spent much of his time pleading cases for immigrants. Then politics drew him away from law. In 1916, La Guardia was elected to the US House of Representatives. In 1933, he became mayor of New York City. During his twelve years in office, La Guardia oversaw the building of playgrounds, parks, and low-cost housing in poor neighborhoods. Today in New York, one of the nation's largest airports bears his name.

Many immigrants leaving Ellis Island didn't go very far. One in three headed straight for New York City across the harbor. New York's towering skyscrapers, noisy streets, and endless activity were a world away from their quiet villages. "The city dazzled us," said one new immigrant. A German boy, William Reinhart, recalled the awe of his first ride on an elevated train. "All of a sudden, [my family of ten] were in the sky! Here we [had been] twenty-one days on the water, and now we were sailing through the sky with water underneath us."

Immigrants settled on blocks filled with people from their own homelands. Such neighborhoods were among the most crowded places in the world. On the Lower East Side, where millions settled over the years, more than four thousand people lived on one block. Their housing was in five- or six-story buildings, called *tenements*. Before, these buildings had held single families. Now up to thirty-two immigrant families squeezed into one. Sometimes ten people slept in a single room.

Since there was little air or sunlight inside, people spilled out onto the streets. Pushcarts and stands lined the sidewalks, selling familiar foods. Immigrants chatted with neighbors in their native language. They had brought some of the Old World to America.

There were US citizens who resented this. They expected the immigrants, who had walked through the nation's open doors, to give up their old ways, speak English, and become full-fledged Americans. This viewpoint, where cultures blended together in one whole, was called the "melting pot."

Child Labor

Across the nation, child labor was common as immigrant youth tried to help their families survive. In 1900, nearly two million children between the ages of five and fourteen worked full-time jobs, usually under terrible conditions. Lewis Hine, one of the photographers at Ellis Island, traveled across America for ten years taking pictures of children in factories and mines. After seeing his photos, Congress began passing laws against child labor in 1916.

Immigrants often faced a great deal of prejudice. Finding a job was especially difficult. In New York, thousands of immigrants worked for very low pay in small factories called "sweatshops." Families also turned their apartments into "home sweatshops," where parents and children worked together day and night. One boy recalled his Scottish family bent over their kitchen table to glue tiny pieces on jewelry. "We'd work until midnight, but never after one. At least I wouldn't, for I had to go to school in the morning."

Over time, the lives of most immigrants improved—especially the children's. Italian immigrant Albertina diGracia recalled: "We were dirt-poor. This country gave us a chance . . . and we worked hard for our children. And now they've got what we worked for. We're satisfied."

Often adult immigrants never learned English or changed their old ways. But their children did—in public schools. In many countries of Europe, only the rich could afford school. In the

United States, school was free and open for every child. Mary Antin, a Russian immigrant, recalled being taken to school after her family moved to a Boston slum. "A little girl from across the alley came and offered to [take] us to school. . . . [There were] no applications made, no questions asked, no examinations . . . no fees. The doors stood open for every one of us."

New arrivals and their luggage

Children playing on the steerage deck of a ship

The steerage deck of a ship

Ferry boats at Ellis Island

Immigrants landing at Ellis Island

Five immigrant women sitting on a dock at Ellis Island

Ellis Island

No. 3163a

A family of Dutch immigrants

Immigrants and their belongings

An exam being given at Ellis Island

A ferry going to Ellis Island

A nineteenth-century print of a wood engraving of immigrants landing at Castle Garden

Immigrants boarding a ferry to Ellis Island

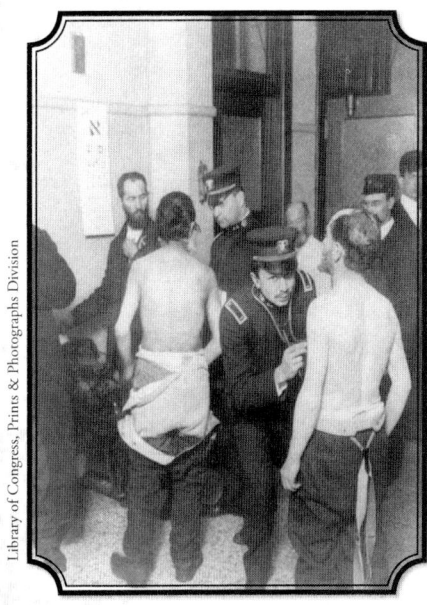

Physicians examining a group of Jewish immigrants

New arrivals in the Immigrant Building

The detention pen

Immigrants on arrival at Ellis Island

An immigrant family at Ellis Island

The large waiting room

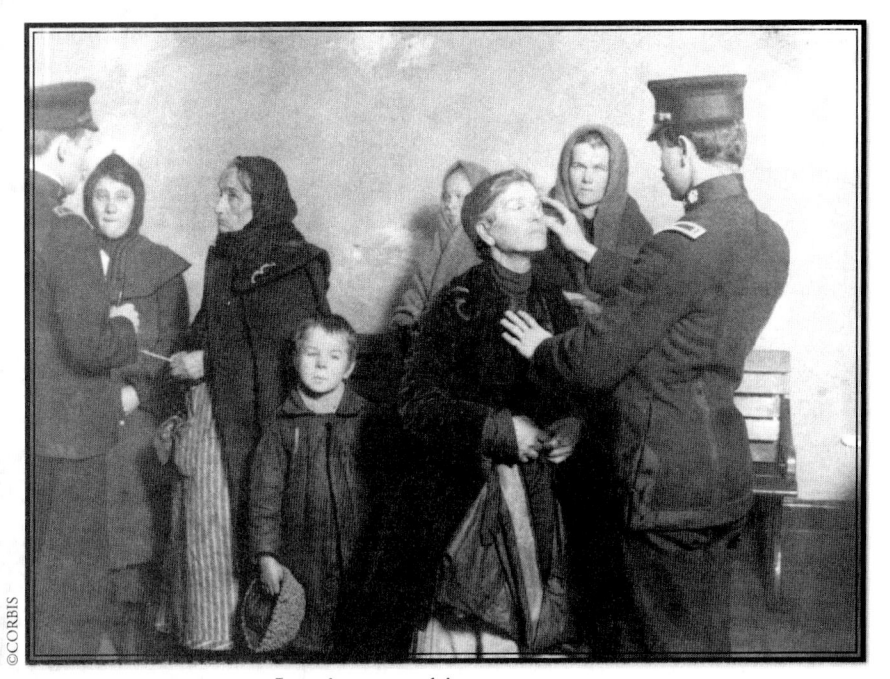

Immigrants taking an eye exam

Immigrant children playing on the rooftop of a school

Irving Berlin

Golda Meir

Young child laborers working at a mill

A five-year-old shrimp-picker

Immigrant children at night school

View from a tenement window

Children playing on a fire escape on the Lower East Side of New York City

A tenement building in New York City

The Great Hall at Ellis Island

An aerial view of Ellis Island

Andrew Carnegie (1835–1919)

Andrew Carnegie was a true rags-to-riches story. Born in Scotland, he came to the United States with his family in 1848 and settled in Pennsylvania. Extreme poverty forced him to begin working full-time in a cotton factory at age thirteen. Yet, in time, he made a fortune in the steel industry and became one of the richest men in the world.

Although Carnegie drove his workers very hard, he was a charitable man in his later years. He believed that the wealthy had a duty to use their money for the common good. Opening free local libraries was one of his favorite causes.

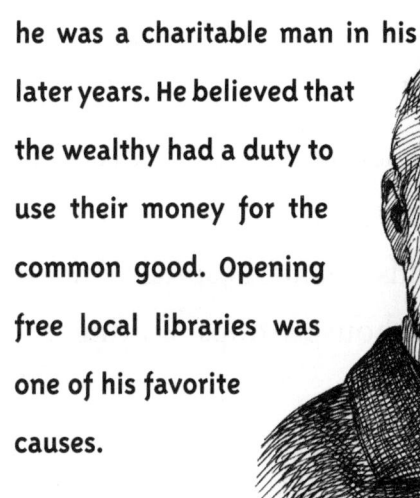

CHAPTER 6
The Open Door Slams Shut

In 1914, World War I began in Europe. It went on for four years. The United States did not join the fighting until 1917. During the war, immigration at Ellis Island slowed to a trickle. In 1914, about 880,000 immigrants had come through its doors. By 1918, the numbers had fallen sharply to 29,000. So, Ellis Island was used for new purposes. During the war, it became a holding pen for enemies of the government. In addition, the army and navy treated their wounded at the Ellis Island hospital. And they used the dorms to house troops waiting to go overseas.

After World War I, the numbers of incoming immigrants soared again. But by this time, a movement against immigration had begun in the United States. Citizens worried about losing jobs to immigrants who would work for lower pay. And prejudice against immigrants was widespread.

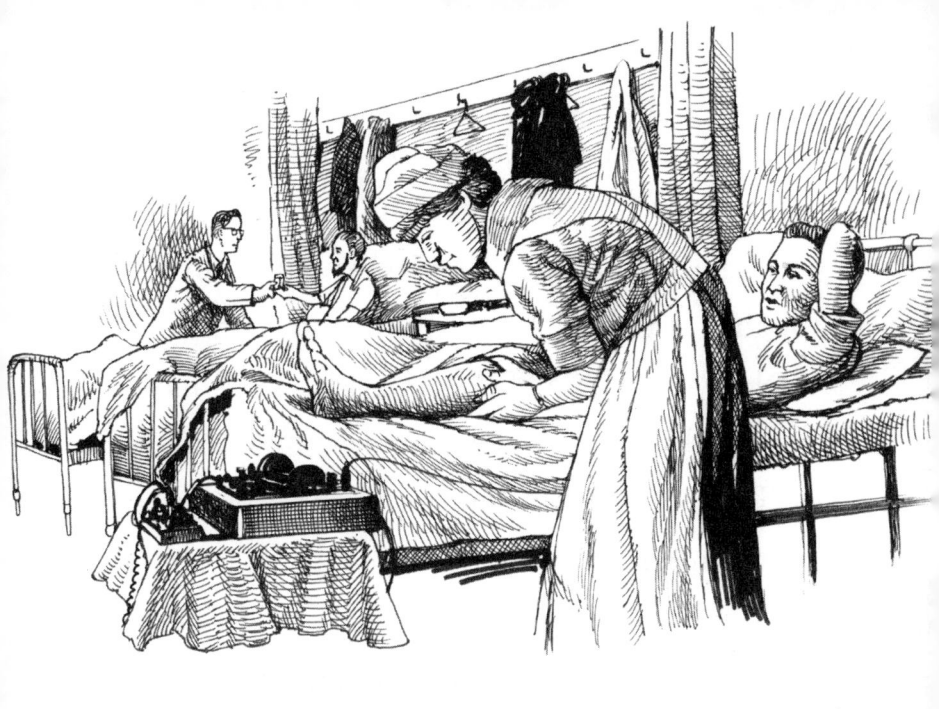

In 1921, Congress passed the Emergency Quota Act. A *quota* means a limit was placed on how many immigrants could enter the United States each year. The number was set at about 350,000. The law also limited how many people could come from each country. Never before had the United States set limits on immigration. The "open door" was slamming shut.

Three years later, in 1924, came an even tougher law. It cut immigration in half. Now a total of about 165,000 immigrants were allowed into the United States each year.

The law also favored people from countries in northern and western Europe. Out of every one hundred immigrants, eighty-five came from these countries. Only twelve of the hundred came from southern and eastern Europe. People from Asia and Africa were left with the remaining three spots.

In 1906, more than 285,000 Italians had come through Ellis Island. The 1921 law limited the number of Italians to 42,000. The 1924 law slashed the number to 4,000 a year.

The law caused yet another major change: It stopped the testing of immigrants at Ellis Island. Testing now took place *before* immigrants left home—at US embassies. These government offices had been set up around the globe after World War I, when the United States became a world power. After 1924, inspectors at Ellis Island just checked the papers of immigrants who came through.

During World War II, Ellis Island was again used to detain foreign enemies and treat wounded servicemen. The US Coast Guard also trained 60,000 troops there.

After the war ended in 1945, most of the buildings lay empty. The cost of keeping the island open was very high. Since the arrival of that Irish girl named Annie Moore, twelve million immigrants had passed through the little island, the gateway to America. Now all those stories were part of history. On November 12, 1954, Ellis Island was closed.

Angel Island

Most immigrants entered the United States through Ellis Island. But there were other immigration stations, too. They were in US ports such as Boston, Baltimore, Miami, and New Orleans. On the West Coast, the most famed immigration station was Angel Island in San Francisco, California. Some called it the "Ellis Island of the West."

About one million immigrants came to Angel Island from 1910 to 1940. Most came from Asia, especially China. The Chinese had started coming to America in large numbers during the California gold rush (1848–1855). In the late 1860s, thousands more came to help build America's first railroads. Since the Chinese worked for very little pay, American workers often resented them. Laws were passed to make it extremely hard for them to enter America. As a result, Angel Island acted mostly as a place to detain and deport immigrants. This was far different than Ellis Island, which passed 98 percent of immigrants into the country. Today, Angel Island is a historic landmark.

CHAPTER 7
Back from Ruins

After 1954, Ellis Island became a ghost town. Buildings, once grand and stately, fell into decay. Weeds and vines overgrew the walls. Windows cracked. Plaster walls crumbled inside. Rain and floods rotted the floors. Thieves snuck onto the deserted island, stealing everything from doorknobs to dishes. Ellis Island was a wreck.

Then, in 1965, President Lyndon Johnson declared Ellis Island a historic site. "For nearly three decades Ellis Island was a . . . symbol of freedom for millions," he said. Johnson put the National Park Service in charge of the site.

The Park Service set about clearing away the junk on the island. Forty thousand tons of garbage were removed. Repairs were made on the Main Building so it was safe for visitors.

In 1976, Ellis Island was opened again to the public for one-hour tours. But the island still looked shabby. *New York Times* writer Sidney H. Schanberg reported on the "slow rot" of the Main Building. "Windows are out, and in one room moss and small trees are growing, and pigeons have settled in."

Bob Hope (1903–2003)

Bob Hope, comedian and actor, kept Americans laughing for most of the twentieth century. In 1903, he was born Leslie Townes Hope in England. When he was four, his family left England in search of the American dream. They came through Ellis Island, where today the Bob Hope Memorial Library stands in his honor. The Hopes settled in Ohio. Bob had successful careers as a stand-up comic, theater actor, and Hollywood movie star. In all his roles he played the funny guy. Starting with World War II, he entertained millions of US troops, bringing humor to war zones all over the world.

Irving Berlin (1888–1989)

Irving Berlin was one of the most popular songwriters of the twentieth century. Besides writing hits like "God Bless America" and "White Christmas," he also wrote many musicals.

He was born Israel Baline in 1888 in Russia. (He later changed his name when it was accidentally misspelled *Berlin* on one of his songs.) His family fled Russia when Irving was five years old, in order to escape the pogroms. After coming through Ellis Island, the family settled in New York City. As a teenager, Irving worked as a street singer and singing waiter. And at nineteen, he published his first song. Irving died at age 101, after writing more than 1,500 songs.

In 1982, the future of Ellis Island looked more promising. President Ronald Reagan set up a special group to find ways to restore the island and turn it into a museum. The cost of restoring Ellis Island was going to cost millions. But the government wouldn't be paying for any of it. The overhaul was to be funded entirely by donations from the American people.

A well-known, successful businessman named Lee Iacocca was put in charge. Iacocca cared deeply about the project. His own parents had come from Italy through Ellis Island. Iacocca raised over $150 million donated by more than twenty million Americans.

The restoration, started in 1984, was a huge challenge. Bringing the Main Building back to its former glory would become the biggest historic restoration job ever done on a building in the United States.

Drying out the building came first. It was so damp inside that two giant heaters had to run nonstop for two years before it dried out. New copper for the four domes replaced the copper stolen by thieves. Amazingly, the prized tile ceiling of the Great Hall needed little repair. The ceiling had been installed in 1917 with over 28,000 tiles. Only twenty-seven of the tiles needed replacing.

As workers scraped paint off the walls, hidden graffiti came to light. Immigrants had scrawled poems, drawings, names, and messages on the walls. What did they write with? They used pencil—and the unforgettable blue chalk of the inspectors! The graffiti was carefully preserved as a piece of living history.

After eight years of work, Ellis Island was ready to open its doors once more.

Golda Meir (1898–1978)

Golda Meir, born Golda Mabovitch, became one of Ellis Island's most famous immigrants.

At age eight, Golda came with her Russian-Jewish family through Ellis Island and settled in Milwaukee, Wisconsin. A born leader, she led fund-raisers to buy schoolbooks for poor classmates. Even though she couldn't speak English when she started school, Golda graduated from junior high at the top of her class.

In college, Golda started working to make Israel a free homeland for Jews. She later moved to Palestine to work for the cause. Israel became an independent nation in 1948; the following year, Golda was the first woman elected to its parliament. One of her roles was to find housing and jobs for 700,000 immigrants arriving in the new state. In 1968, Golda was elected prime minister of Israel. True to her own immigrant past, Golda opened Israel's doors to people of other nations.

CHAPTER 8
Ellis Island Today

On September 10, 1990, Ellis Island's doors reopened. Now the Main Building was a museum.

Its purpose was to "recall the human drama that occurred within these walls."

Today the Ellis Island National Monument is one of the most popular historic landmarks in the country. It's not surprising.

The two million people who visit each year arrive by ferry—just as the immigrants did.

Then they follow the immigrants' footsteps into the Baggage Room of the Main Building. It looks the way it did in the 1910s. Trunks, suitcases, and cloth bags are piled about, tagged with numbers from the ships' manifests.

Visitors then climb the stairway where doctors once carefully watched immigrants for signs of bad health. Upstairs they enter the giant space of the Great Hall. The voices of immigrants can be heard over loudspeakers, speaking about their experiences. In smaller rooms, visitors see where detainees ate, slept, and waited.

On view are belongings of past immigrants—landing cards, photographs, children's toys, clothes, and more. An interactive exhibit contains old manifest records from the ships that immigrants sailed on. Anyone can look through them to discover relatives. Today four out of ten

Americans can trace their family history back to Ellis Island. (If you have family members who went through Ellis Island, you can view their manifest records online at http://www.ellisisland.org.)

At present, immigrants are once again coming to America in great numbers. For many years, the number of immigrants has topped one million. People come to America for the same reasons as before. Behind them lie war, prejudice, and poverty. Ahead of them lies the American dream.

In 1965, Congress ended quotas set on countries. However, limits on total immigration remain in place. The laws are always changing. American citizens still debate the larger questions of immigration. What limits should there be? Who should be allowed to enter the country? How Americans answer those questions decides who we are.

Most monuments honor a famous person.

Not Ellis Island. The Ellis Island National Monument honors ordinary people. Millions of them passed through this small island in New York Harbor and went on to help build the United States.

Photographers

Over the years, photographers were drawn to Ellis Island to take pictures of immigrants. Augustus Sherman, who worked at Ellis Island, captured more than two hundred portraits of immigrants, many of them wearing their native clothes. Most likely, the people who posed for him were being detained on the island. Today a number of Sherman's portraits hang in the Ellis Island Immigration Museum.

Timeline of Ellis Island

1776	Around this time, Samuel Ellis buys the island that will bear on his name from then on
1808	The US government buys Ellis Island
1855	Castle Garden, at the tip of New York City, opens to admit immigrants
1890	The federal government takes over control of immigration from individual states
	Building of the first immigration station begins on Ellis Island. The island's size is doubled
1897	On June 15, a fire completely destroys the island's wood buildings
1900	On December 17, the present brick and stone Main Building opens
1907	In this peak year of immigration, 1,285,349 immigrants pass through Ellis Island
1917	Ellis Island is used to detain enemies during World War I
1921	The Emergency Quota Act limits the number of immigrants to America
1941	Ellis Island serves as a detainment center and training grounds during World War II
1954	On November 12, Ellis Island officially closes
1976	Ellis Island is opened for tours, but the island is badly rundown
1990	The Ellis Island Immigration Museum opens in the restored Main Building

Timeline of the World

The Revolutionary War is fought from 1775–1783	1775
The Irish Potato Famine begins	1845
The Statue of Liberty, a gift from France, is stationed in New York Harbor	1886
From 1903–1906, pogroms in Russia kill thousands of Jews	1903
Angel Island Immigration Station opens in San Francisco Bay to admit Asian immigrants	1910
Government in Turkey murders 1.5 million Armenians from 1915 to 1923. A half million escape to America.	1915
The United States enters World War I	1917
Alexander Fleming discovers penicillin	1928
On December 7, Pearl Harbor is attacked and America enters World War II	1941
Immigration Act of 1965 ends quota laws	1965

Bibliography

*Books for young readers

Cannato, Vincent J. *American Passage: The History of Ellis Island.* New York: HarperCollins Publishers, 2009.

*Landau, Elaine. *Ellis Island (A True Book).* New York: Children's Press, 2008.

*McDaniel, Melissa. *Ellis Island (Cornerstones of Freedom).* New York: Children's Press, 2012.

*Rebman, Renee C. *Life on Ellis Island.* San Diego: Lucent Books, 2000.

Reeves, Pamela. *Ellis Island: Gateway to the American Dream.* New York: Michael Friedman Publishing Group, Inc., 1991.

*Sandler, Martin W. *Island of Hope: The Story of Ellis Island and the Journey to America.* New York: Scholastic, Inc., 2004.

*Staton, Hilarie. *Ellis Island (Symbols of American Freedom).* New York: Chelsea House Publishers, 2010.

Websites

Svejda, Dr. George J. "Castle Garden As an Immigrant Depot, 1855–1890." Office of Archeology and Historic Preservation, National Park Service. December 2, 1968. Retrieved March 22, 2013, from **nps.gov/history/history/online_books/elis/castle_garden.pdf**.

"The Statue of Liberty-Ellis Island Foundation, Inc." Retrieved March 22, 2013, from www.ellisisland.org.